The
George W. Bush
Joke Book
★
(UNCENSORED)

The George W. Bush Joke Book

(UNCENSORED)

Written and compiled by

Nelson David

Robson Books

This edition first published in 2001 by Robson Books,
10 Blenheim Court, Brewery Road, London N7 9NY

A member of the Chrysalis Group plc

British Library Cataloguing in Publication Data
A catalogue record for this title is available from the British
Library.

ISBN 1 86105 478 5

Typeset by FiSH Books, London WC1
Printed by Creative Print & Design (Wales), Ebbw Vale

CONTENTS

v

For Sue Bennett with love

FOREWORD

This book was written over the summer of 2001, before America's terrible tragedy of September 11th. So much has been written about that awful event and here is not the appropriate place to add to the chorus. Instead my job, as a satirist, is to continue to heckle the rich and powerful. That was always the purpose of this book – and it remains so. To remind the great and the good that maybe they're not so great and good after all. In particular, the 'great' man at the centre of our attention is former Oil Magnate now 'President' of the USA George W Bush. Some men are born great, some have greatness thrust upon them – Dubya is still waiting. Freud was the first to observe that in difficult times, humour is often a good way to deal with hidden fears and difficult emotions, providing a pipeline to the subconscious. Which leads us to the amazing discovery that President Bush actually has something in common with the intellectual genius Sigmund Freud – they're both experts on buried pipelines.

I'd like to thank Iain Dale for inspiring the idea, everyone whose material is reproduced in the quotes section, Melanie Letts for her kind encouragement, Natalie Jerome for expert guidance and – especially – Jeremy Robson for being a man of his word.

Peace and love

P.S. Everything that George Bush actually says (indicated in *italics* followed by his initials) is actually written. Many don't make sense, but when you're the most powerful man in the world, it seems that you can say pretty much what you want!

Nelson David (editor www.spin-on-this.com)
November 2001

1

THE OILIGARCHY

Who's who in the world of George W. Bush

George W. Bush 43rd President of the USA

George W. Bush is just like JFK – a millionaire Ivy League playboy with a powerful dad. Though in fairness President Kennedy did win the election using the traditional method of actually getting more votes than his opponent, Richard Nixon! Dubya, as he is sometimes known, was raised in Texas where he owned a baseball team and ran a petrol company. Some have criticised the way Bush runs the USA for the benefit of his corporate backers. But, as they say in American politics, 'you dance with them what brung yer.'

George H. W. Bush

It is claimed that the Bush clan are distantly related to the British Royal Family. But despite enjoying the comparisons, George Senior once said, 'We are not a dynasty, my job is not a legacy.' In Dubya's case not so much a legacy – more a liability.

Barbara Bush

Little George's mum Barbara is regarded as the rock of the Bush dynasty. And, let's be honest, no-one was better qualified than Barbara to help iron out life's little wrinkles.

Laura Bush

Used to be an infant teacher. Her experience as a patient woman helping the clueless to read, write and get a grip on the realities of life was perfect preparation for marriage to George W. Bush.

The Twins (Jenna and Barbara)

George W. like Britain's own dear Tony Blair, is fiercely protective of his children and made sure they were never public tabloid fodder. Until that little bit of business with a fake ID and some bottles of beer. Kids eh? I blame the parents.

Jeb Bush

George's kid brother, Governor of Florida. He oversaw the recount which turned plain old Dubya into President Bush. Jeb insists that during the recount, everything was above board. Apart from the Democrats votes obviously, which were under the table.

Katherine Harris

Florida Secretary of State who played a crucial role in the 2000 American election. Known as the 'brassy lassie from Tallahassee', Katherine had to endure many cruel taunts. For example her paint-by-numbers make-up, led to cries of a recount!

Dick Cheney

Should be renamed RoboVeep. Known for having major heart surgery then popping straight back to the Oval Office. Renowned lazybones Bush once said that he'd like to clone Vice President Cheney so that he could do even less work. Cheney used his time out of office (between Dad and Dubya) profitably by becoming the multi-millionaire boss of Halliburton, a worldwide oil corporation. When it was thought Dick might need a pig's heart loyal Dubya instantly offered to go and stick one for him.

Condoleezza Rice

Bush's National Security Adviser used to sit on the board of Chevron Oil Company and – this is not a joke – they liked her so much they named an oil tanker after her. Presumably that's why they say she's the one who can keep Bush on an even keel.

Karl Rove

One of Dubya's top publicity strategists. Before becoming Bush's press man, Karl used to work for Big Tobacco. His job was to spin good news for an organisation that polluted the atmosphere and made people sick – so now you know why Dubya hired him.

Donald Rumsfeld

When Dubya created his 'best of the Cold War cabinet' it was like some old dinosaur rock group making an unwanted comeback. There's Cheney on vocals, Powell on lead guitar, and right at the back the quietly sinister bass man 'Rummy' Rumsfeld. But beware. When Defence boss Rummy yells to the crowd 'We're gonna take the roof off this place!' he's not talking about music but his plans to deploy the new Exoatmospheric Kill Vehicle Missile System.

Colin Powell

Secretary of State. Colin's job is to make sure George W. Bush doesn't start World War Three – at least not until everyone's on board. Ironic that Gulf War veteran Powell is seen as the dove, while Dubya – a man who never quite made it to Vietnam – comes on like Rambo in a suit.

Texas

Former Texas Governor George W. Bush, despite his massively privileged upbringing, has done a good job of convincing millions he's 'a good ole boy, up from the country and jes passin thru' y all!' Don't be fooled.

Texas is a massive state (pop. approx. 20 million) and home to some of the most powerful corporations in the world. But it's not true they constantly ring up Dubya instructing him how to run the country – no need, they pop round and tell him in person.

Al Gore

Remember him? He's the one who got more votes than Bush but lost. However, instead of sympathy they just makes jokes about the poor old sap. What's the difference between a puppy and Al Gore? After two months the puppy opens its eyes and stops whining.

George W. Bush School Report – previously unseen

GENERAL NOTES
Little George finds it hard to keep up with the other children yet in some ways is strangely precocious. At school sports day when we gave him an egg and spoon he used them to make a hangover cure.

Politics
Needs to try harder. Apparently thinks manual recount is a Mexican revolutionary.

English
No one uses the language quite like George. His essay 'What Did I on Holidays My Summer' was the talk of the school for weeks.

Geography
George recently saw a map with the words 'You Are Here' – he got rather paranoid, burst into tears and said 'Miss, who told them I was coming?'

Biology
Very interested when we dissected a frog in class. Said the incision reminded him of a scar his friend little Dick Cheney had shown him.

Physics
George hooked up the classroom chairs to a Van Der Graaf generator. This was inexcusable and explaining everything to the bereaved parents was a nightmare.

History
When asked to define history, George keeps grinning and saying 'the Commies!'

Chemistry
George puzzles us. He was very keen to experiment with chemical substances in class. However, when the others wanted to join in he told them 'just say no kids.'

Foreign Languages
See English.

Maths
Fuzzy. George must remember Pythagoras is not some Grecian towelhead, logarithms are not what lumberjacks do on the dance floor, and algebra is not the Little Mermaid's underwear.

2

DUMB AND DUBYA

It's the President stupid

Child: *What is the White House like?*
GWB: *It's white.*

George W. Bush is really really nervous about his first meeting with the Pope. But after the introductions, the Pope seems very friendly and says to George, 'Tell me – there's something I've always wanted to know. What does the 'W' stand for in George W. Bush?'

Dubya explains 'It stands for Walker sir, your Holiness.'

Thank you my son,' says the Pope.

'No problem your Eminence,' replies Bush, relieved that things have got off to such a good start. 'In fact, your Holiness, you've reminded me of something I've always wanted to ask you. Tell me sir, what does the 'H' stand for in Jesus H. Christ?'

George W. Bush was taken to the British Library reading room and asked if he wanted to see the autograph of Charles Dickens. Bush looked excited 'You bet – any chance he could sign it to George, Laura and the twins?'

Q: Why is George W. Bush no good at snooker?
A: He won't come out until the reds have gone.

In the State of Texas there are actually official instructions on how to salute the flag. And when George W. Bush was Governor apparently there were also instructions on how to pronounce it.

Q: How did George W. Bush prove his ignorance?
A: He failed a DNA test.

White House staff soon realised George W. Bush isn't best blessed in the brains department – first day at work he bought a corner table for the Oval Office.

'We want our teachers to be trained so they can meet their obligations, their obligations as teachers. We want them to know how to teach the science of reading. In order to make sure there's not this kind of federal federal cufflink.' GWB

Q: What do you get when you cross a Stepford Wife with Forrest Gump?
A: Barbara and Jenna.

George W. Bush went to Lapland and told the Prime Minister – 'You Lapps are a wonderful people. I especially love your dancers.'

When George W. Bush went to Rome they asked him what he thought of the Sistine – 'Great! I pulled the handle and it flushed just like the ones back in Texas.'

George W. Bush was asked what action should be taken with Slobodan Milosevic – 'Easy, make him change his name to Bob.'

Q: What did George W. Bush get out of Yale University?
A: He got out of studying, he got out of exams – but mainly he got out of his skull.

'What's not fine is, rarely is the question asked, are, is our children learning.' GWB

George W. Bush was in Italy on a State visit when Berlusconi said 'Tomorrow, George, we're taking you to the Leaning Tower of Pisa.' Dubya said 'Why? Don't you have a Domino Pizza?'

Of all American presidents, George W. Bush has the most trouble with culture. Someone bought him tickets for *Swan Lake* – and he took his fishing rods.

Q: What's the difference between a tapestry maker and George W. Bush?
A: A tapestry maker can string a sentence together.

Dick Cheney took George W. Bush to a concert hall to see Beethoven's Fifth. Dubya was so disappointed when he realised it wasn't a sequel to the dog movie.

George W. Bush was taken to the British Library reading room and told it was where Marx wrote his greatest works. Bush looked impressed, 'Groucho, Chico or Harpo?'

'My education message will resignate amongst all parents.' GWB

George W. Bush went to Italy and was asked if he was a fan of opera. 'Hell no,' he said, 'She's nowhere near as good as Jerry Springer.'

Tony Blair invited George W. Bush to stay with him. Blair asked, 'Would you like to spend the day at Chequers?' Bush replied 'Couldn't we play frisbee instead?'

George W. Bush was attending a summit in Italy. As he dipped his ciabbata in the olive oil he turned to Berlusconi – 'This stuff tastes great. Do you drill for it locally?'

Journalists asked George W. Bush what measures he'd take to stop the spate of gun massacres in schools. 'Easy – we gotta tell those kids to start using blanks.'

Dick Cheney took George W. Bush to a French restaurant. The wine waiter asked 'Red or white?' Dubya replied, 'I ain't dumb – let's see the other colours, then I'll choose...'

'There is a lot of speculation and I guess there is going to continue to be a lot of speculation until the speculation ends.' GWB

George W. Bush was arrested for drink-driving. The magistrate said, 'Mr Bush, I'm going to pronounce your sentence.' Dubya replied, 'Thank God, Your Honour – if I tried we'd be here all week!'

Colin Powell was talking to a journalist about Dubya's lack of foreign policy knowledge. 'Jeez it gets embarrassing. Last week he tried to send his laundry to the Ethnic Cleansers.'

George W. Bush enjoyed his first trip to Rome. He was asked to light a candle for the Pope – 'Hell I can do better than that – I'm buying the old guy oil-powered central heating.'

George W. Bush isn't brilliant at languages. In his English class at Andover the teacher asked 'George, what's the best way to end a sentence?'
George thought for a minute and smiled hopefully, 'The electric chair?'

Bush was being interviewed by a journalist. He was asked if he thought whether, in the world of global capitalism, brands were getting too big. 'Nah mine's on my buttocks and you can hardly see it,'

'*More and more of our imports come from overseas.*'
GWB

Q: What's the difference between George W. Bush and Tolstoy's *War and Peace*?
A: *War and Peace* is thick but you don't want to put it down.

George W. Bush was asked by his Maths lecturer, 'What can you tell me about the square on the hypotenuse?' He replied, 'Is it Al Gore?'

George W. Bush insists he used his time at Yale University wisely. In fact he loved nothing better than to lock himself away and study his favourite historical characters – Jim Beam, Jack Daniels and the Marlboro man.

Dubya doesn't spend too much time at the theatre. He thinks Shakespeare is the first rule of Pig Sticking.

Back in his drinking days George W. Bush woke up one morning and realised his wallet was empty. The night before he'd had 200 dollars in it. He drove down to the bar and asked the bartender 'Did I spend 200 dollars in here last night?'

'You sure did. Bought drinks for everyone in the place twice over,' he replied.

Dubya looked relieved. 'Thank God for that – I thought I'd lost it!'

Dick Cheney took Dubya to see an art house movie in New York. After, Dick asked George, 'Did you follow the subtext?' George said, 'No, I came in the limo as usual.'

'*You teach a child to read, and he or her will be able to pass a literacy test.*' GWB

Dubya was asked if he'd ever seen *King Lear*. 'Sure – Benny Hill is my favourite comedian.'

Bush was asked by a group of students, 'What do you think of Plato's *Republic*?' Bush thought for a long while, smiled and said, 'I'm looking forward to visiting it on my next European tour.'

George W. Bush was asked what he thought of the problem of illiteracy among the poor – 'I've made it clear, I think folk should marry before they have kids.'

There was one awkward moment when George W. Bush was being shown round the Vatican by the Pope. Dubya asked, 'Where's the john?' The Pope replied 'I'm here.'

Q: Why did Pillsbury want George W. Bush to join the Dough Boy in their next TV ad?
A: Because two half-baked heads are better than one.

'I understand small business growth. I was one.'
GWB

3

HAIL TO THE THIEF!

'President' of the USA

'If you don't stand for anything, you don't stand for anything. If you don't stand for something, you don't stand for anything.' GWB

George W. Bush says the election that made him President of the USA was a stunning example of people power. 'Sure was. I rang my people – they put me in power!'

Q: What's the connection between Diana Ross and George W. Bush?
A: They couldn't have done it without the Supremes.

George W. Bush spends so much time on the golf course, White House insiders are worried it muddles his head on matters of state. Last week he spent two hours trying to chip his way out of a nuclear bunker.

The good news is George W. Bush has his finger on the pulse – the bad news is the pulse is Dick Cheney's.

Q: What is George W. Bush's traffic policy?
A: Jam today and jam tomorrow.

Q: What's the easiest way to get up George W. Bush's backside?
A: Hang on to Tony Blair's legs.

George W. Bush says he gave up drinking on his fortieth birthday – but apparently before that he was known as the 51st state.

George W. Bush got really nervous when he heard Tony Blair was going to give him a sculpture of Winston Churchill. Last time someone organised a bust for him he ended up in front of a magistrate.

'*The new Prime Minister of India is . . . no.*' GWB

Dick Cheney had just left hospital after a heart attack and George W. Bush was surprised to receive a goodwill card and gift delivered by hand from Saddam Hussein. The card said, 'Whatever's gone on between us I want to show Dick there's no hard feelings. I hope he makes a full recovery and enjoys

this all-American gift.' Bush opened the box to find five buckets of KFC wings, a pack of Dunkin' Donuts and tub of Häagen-Dazs.

Journalists were puzled when George W. Bush said the thing he had in common with Tony Blair was Colgate toothpaste. Asked how he knew this Bush said, 'Easy – first thing Tony reached for after kissing my ass!'

George W. Bush is glad his heavy drinking days are behind him. It was awful having glazed eyes, not being able to speak properly and looking such an idiot – and the drinking just made it worse.

'*I will have a foreign handed foreign policy.*' GWB

Q: What's the difference between George W. Bush and Quasimodo?
A: One's an ugly retard famous for his clangers – the other's a sympathetic character from French fiction.

After Cheney had his pacemaker fitted George W. Bush visited him in hospital. 'Dick, there's good news and bad news. Good news is it works perfectly – bad news is it runs on batteries not petrol.'

George W. Bush got a little bit jealous when he heard his national security adviser Condoleezza Rice had had a 130,000 ton oil tanker named after her. Colin Powell took him aside and said, 'Don't be down-hearted George. I happen to know there's already a vehicle that's been named in your honour.'
Dubya's eyes lit up, 'Really?'
'Sure – the Dump truck.'

Q: What's the difference between George W. Bush and a rotovator?
A: The rotovator doesn't grin while it's screwing the planet.

Q: Why did Dick Cheney say working with Dubya was good preparation for having a heart attack?
A: Because that constant pain in the chest made a nice change from a constant pain in the arse.

Q: What's the difference between JFK and George W. Bush?
A: It used to take a lot more than two shots to get Dubya out of his skull.

Q: What's the difference between Vice President Cheney and Bill Clinton?
A: Clinton never needed any help with his pumping organ.

George W. Bush insists he was the clear winner in the American election, 'Anyone who disagrees needs their chads examined.'

Q: What car does George W. Bush like to drive when he's in Dallas?
A: Anything with a roof.

'We'll let our friends be the peacekeepers and the great country called America will be the pacemakers.' GWB

The good news is George W. Bush is a man of his word – the bad news is no-one can find that word in the dictionary.

Q: Why do people take an instant dislike to George W. Bush?
A: It saves time.

George W. Bush is the first American President who thinks Guns'n'Roses is a wedding anniversary shopping list.

In April 2001 President George W. Bush celebrated his first 100 days and Jenna celebrated her first 100 Tequilas.

Someone asked George W. Bush, 'How can you possibly sign a death warrant to take away someone's life?' Bush replied, 'It was easy – 'specially after Laura taught me how to write my name!'

'This is still a dangerous world. It's a world of madmen and uncertainty and potential mential losses.' GWB

Tony Blair gave George W. Bush a statue of Winston Churchill. 'He's the greatest Tory leader Britain ever had,' says Bush. Laura replies, 'I know who Tony Blair is honey.'

Q: Why did Clinton like foreign policy business more than George W. Bush?
A: Because he couldn't resist abroad.

Q: Why is Dick Cheney the world's most brilliant soldier?
A: He's the only man who didn't serve in Vietnam but still got a purple heart.

Dubya's advisers are briefing him about the Chinese. 'How does this Communism work?' asks Bush. Rumsfeld explains, 'Well, the government is

unelected. They lie to the population. And the country is run in the interests of a small elite who cream off all the goodies.' Bush looks at Rumsfeld and says, 'Bastards – who sold them our State secrets?'

Q: What has George W. Bush been advised to do if Dick Cheney ever experiences another cardio-vascular dysfunction?
A: Get someone else to pronounce it.

As soon as Cheney had his pacemaker fitted doctors told him he'd need to be hooked up with a drip. Cheney said, 'You bet – I want to get back working with President Bush as soon as possible.'

Q: Why won't George W. Bush change a light bulb?
A: It's not often he's in a room with something dimmer than he is.

'Keep good relations with the Grecians.' GWB

Q: What's the difference between George W. Bush and a deer in the headlights?
A: You'd stop the car for a deer.

Q: Why did George W. Bush cross the road?
A: To prove to the traffic cop he could walk straight.

Q: Why do the press think George W. Bush once took drugs?
A: Because of all the people shouting, 'Look at that dope in the Whitehouse!'

Q: Why is George W. Bush like the American flag?
A: Doesn't matter if he's flapping – someone else is pulling the strings.

Q: What's the difference between George W. Bush and Abe Lincoln?
A: You wouldn't catch Dubya dead in a theatre.

'If this were a dictatorship it'd be a heck of a lot easier, just so long as I'm the dictator.' GWB

The White House is America's most important historic building and no expense is spared to make sure it remains in immaculate condition. Since Dubya arrived in office, the White House lawn is sprinkled every night. Though one of these days when dad finds out, Jenna's going to be in big trouble.

Q: What's the connection between a prisoner on death row and Dubya's brain?
A: One lonely cell.

Q: Why are there more assassinations in the USA than anywhere else?
A: Because in the American Dream, everyone gets a shot at the Presidency.

Q: What's the difference between George W. Bush and Bill Clinton?
A: At least Clinton admitted he was ruled by his Dick.

Q: What's the biggest change since Dubya gave up drinking?
A: His finger's on the button and we're the ones pissing our pants.

Q: How many Dick Cheneys does it take to change a light bulb?
A: Forget the light bulb – re-route that socket to Dick's chest NOW!'

As a supporter of the religious right, George W. Bush has come up with a sure-fire way to decrease the amount of sex, drugs and violence in Hollywood – he's refused point blank to sell them the rights to his life story.

Q: What's the difference between a Clinton intern and a George W. Bush intern?
A: Dubya's interns don't suck up to the boss.

Q: What's the difference between George W. Bush and Saddam Hussein?
A: One's an unelected dictator who signs death warrants – the other's that Iraqi bloke with a 'tache.

Q: What's the difference between George W. Bush and Bill Clinton?
A: George finds it impossible to get his tongue round little teasers.

Q: How many Jenna Bushes does it take to change a light bulb?
A: Two. One to change the light bulb, one to explain everything to the cops.

Q: What do you call an American plane that's just returned from China?
A: Airfix One.

White House staff say things have changed since Dubya took over from Clinton – he has instigated daily prayer meetings. 'In the old days, it wasn't the one kneeling who shouted, "Oh God! Oh God!"'

Q: How did Dubya quit binge drinking?
A: He started signing death warrants and watched others getting slaughtered instead.

'There's no question that the minute I got elected, the storm clouds on the horizon were getting nearly directly overhead.' GWB

Q: How many Californians does it take to change a light bulb?
A: It's not the light bulb – it's another power cut.

To be fair, George W. Bush was very gracious when he became President of the United States. As he said, 'It's time to set aside our differences and give a big hand to the plucky loser – me!'

George W. Bush and Dick Cheney were out at a restaurant in Washington. After studying the menu the waiter said, 'The stuffed heart is excellent today.' Bush replied, 'That's why we made him Vice President.'

George W. Bush used to have a drink problem but says there was one book that helped him through it all, 'Sure – the Oddbins catalogue!'

Q: What's the difference between George W. Bush and Air Force One?
A: One burns petrol, pollutes the environment and causes people to put their hands over their ears . . . the other's a plane.

'A tax cut is really one of the anecdotes to coming out of an economic illness.' GWB

Ever since Dick Cheney had open heart surgery, George W. Bush always makes sure Dick's the man in charge of catering at White House barbecues. 'That's 'cos Dick's ribs are always real tender!'

George W. Bush was very impressed when he moved into the White House. There was a sign on the lawn saying 'Keep off the grass.' Bush says, 'Nice of Clinton to leave a reminder.'

Q: How do we know Tony Blair's son fancies Dubya's daughters?
A: Because he dreamt about going to a party and waking up next morning in a bush.

George Bush Senior once said he would only ever consider being in the Republican Party. President George W. Bush once said he was wholly committed to the Republican Party. And Jenna Bush once said, 'Who gives a shit whose party it is – all I need to know is where's the free bar?'

Q: Why didn't George W. Bush have to dodge the draft?
A: He was too busy drinking it.

When Dubya moved into the White House he was amazed at just how historic the building was. His first surprise was discovering the cornerstone of the building was laid in 1792. His second surprise was discovering it wasn't laid by Bill Clinton.

People say it's just as well George W. Bush gave up drinking before moving into the White House –
no-one wants a President who's paranoid, aggressive and thinks the whole world is against him.

'People shouldn't read into venue locations into someone's heart.' GWB

Q: What's the connection between George W. Bush trying to look Presidential and the Washington Hospital Coronary Unit?
A: They both leave Dick Cheney in stitches.

George W. Bush says despite his privileged background he believes in equal opportunities. 'And as a kid my family practised what we preached. If I remember rightly, all our servants were black.'

Q: What was Dubya's most solemn promise to those who put him in power?
A: A receipt.

Q: Why does George W. Bush call Dick Cheney 'a treasure'?
A: Because they bury him in paperwork and open up his chest.

George W. Bush was in conversation with Queen Elizabeth II. 'I'm really fascinated to know how your people accept being ruled by an unelected hereditary Head of State?' asked the Queen.

'I know what I believe. I will continue to articulate what I believe and what I believe – I believe that what I believe is right.' **GWB**

After Dick Cheney had his heart attack George W. Bush heard he was planning a by-pass. 'Typical Dick, anything to increase petrol sales!'

George W. Bush says he believes in minority rights. 'Sure do. That's why we made sure the Republicans won the election.'

4

ICH BIN EIN OIL TANKER

The adventures of 'Burning' Bush

'I know the human being and the fish can coexist peacefully.' GWB

Q: How can you tell George W. Bush is an oil man?
A: He's thick, crude and easily bored.

George W. Bush reckons if it makes a profit, who cares about the environmental effect? He's the only man in history who sold his family tree to a multi-national logging company.

Q: Why is George W. Bush no good at golf?
A: He spends the entire game trying to avoid the Greens.

Bush was criticised at a press conference for his obsession with oil. 'Look, I believe in renewable energy – and let's face it folks, what's more renewable than a tank of petrol!'

Q: How can you tell when Jenna is on Air Force One?
A: It's not just the plane that enjoys turbo-charged refuelling.

George W. Bush insists that deep down he's Green. 'It's true. I want nothing more than to see the earth completely covered in beautiful plants – steel plants, oil plants, nuclear plants...'

Q: What does George W. Bush plan to do about increased Global Warming floods?
A: Buy a bigger speedboat.

'Natural gas is hemispheric. I like to call it hemispheric in nature because it is a product that we can find in our neighbourhoods.' GWB

Q: Why does George W. Bush get along so well with ExxonMobil?
A: Because he used to get tanked up and piss on the local environment too.

People don't realise, but George W. Bush really is environmentally friendly – whenever he rips up an international treaty he always throws it in the recycle bin.

48

George W. Bush's California energy policy makes him a truly miraculous President. He's the only American in history who gave up drinking then started getting regular blackouts.

George W. Bush really loves flying on Air Force One. Nothing to with the prestige of having a Presidential plane – it's just every time they refuel he gets a royalty.

George W. Bush insists that despite appearances he really is environmentally aware. 'Sure I am. I traded in my ten gallon hat for a five gallon one instead.'

Someone asked George W. Bush why he thought the Cold War ended. He replied nervously, 'Global warming?'

'But I also made it clear to (Vladimir Putin) that it's important to think beyond the old days of when we had the concept that if we blew each other up, the world would be safe.' GWB

Q: How can George W. Bush reduce toxic emissions
A: 'Easy, I'll tell Jenna to stick to soft drinks.'

Q: What's the difference between Saddam Hussein
and George W. Bush?
A: It took Saddam twenty years to get that
unpopular.

George W. Bush has a quick response for advisers
who tell him the world's not prepared to pay such a
terrible price for petrol pollution. 'OK, so offer the
assholes a discount.'

George W. Bush was asked about American
corporations logging in National Forests, 'What's
going to happen about oxygenation?' Bush replied,
'They can apply for a UN grant just like any other
nation.'

Jenna Bush told her dad she wanted to go Green. He
said, 'Carry on drinking like that honey and believe
me you will.'

'This is Preservation Month. I appreciate preservation. It's what you do when you run for President. You gotta preserve.' GWB

George W. Bush was told about Jose Bové, the environmentalist who dumped manure inside a French McDonalds. Says Bush, 'That's not right. It's elected politicians who are supposed to make their points with bullshit.'

Q: What's the connection between George W. Bush and Bill Clinton?
A: They've both spent their lives drilling for days waiting for the big spurt to happen.

Dick Cheney was coming round from having his pacemaker fitted. The doctor said, 'There's good news and bad news. Good news is the pacemaker's working – bad news is it's plugged into the Californian power grid.'

George W. Bush may consider a National Recycling Programme. 'Well we've gotta do something to clear the bottles outta Jenna's bedroom.'

Q: What was the first giveaway sign that George W. Bush is a warmonger?
A: He tried to sell ballistic missiles to the Salvation Army.

'I killed a killdee, I thought was a dove ... I'm glad it wasn't deer season, I might have killed a cow.' GWB

Q: Why do they call George W. Bush the Big Oil President?
A: Because they scraped the bottom of the barrel to find him.

Dubya met with advisers to talk about germ warfare. 'What do you want us to do about weapons which use chemicals from bacteria?' Bush replied instantly, 'Easy. Go to the Balkans and bomb those freakin' Bacterians till they stop supplying them.'

When it comes to the environment George W. Bush is a President prepared to put his foot down. 'Absolutely. The limos burn up gas so much quicker that way!'

Q: What's the difference between Dick Cheney and the Alaskan National Park?
A: There's usually a bit of life left in Cheney when they finish excavating.

Q: How can you tell George W. Bush is an oil man?
A: Even his elections are rigged.

George W. Bush was heckled by environmental protestors shouting, 'We need concrete proposals on the environment!' Bush yelled back, 'I've got concrete proposals – 50 new freeways!'

'Well I think if you say you're going to do something and don't do it, that's trustworthiness.' GWB

Q: What's the difference between George W. Bush and Bill Clinton?
A: When Bush says, 'Hi girls, take a look at my big shiny pumping nozzle and let me fill you up,' he means petrol.

A group of journalists were quizzing George W. Bush about GM foods. 'Mr Bush, what are the main advantages of GM tomatoes?' Bush replies, 'Simple. Everyone gets a leg.'

Desperate protestors asked George W. Bush, 'When it comes to the environment, will you ever have a change of heart?' Bush says, 'No way. I'll leave that to Cheney!'

George W. Bush has a standard answer to people worried his new missile system means he could bomb any town centre on the planet, 'Come on. Doesn't everyone welcome a boom in the high street!'

When Dubya arrived at the White House he asked Cheney to organise an emergency drill. 'You never know when we may need it to dig up the lawn for oil.'

Q: How can you tell Dubya's committed to wind power?
A: His first words to environmentalists are always 'blow it out your ass.'

'When I was coming up it was a dangerous world and you knew exactly who they were. It was us versus them and it was clear who them was. Today, we are not so sure who they are, but we know they're there.' **GWB**

5

TOP 11 LISTS

(Counted by Jeb)

'Anyway I'm so thankful, and so gracious – I'm gracious that my brother Jeb is concerned 'bout the hemisphere as well.' **GWB**

Quotes George W. Bush hasn't made...YET

'I admit – I was privileged. I had the best education money can squander.'

'Dyslexia is no lunching matter.'

'My fellow Albanians.'

'I believe in hard work – I just wouldn't wanna live there!'

'It's just not true to say this county is run by Big Business in the interests of Big Business. That's my job.'

'What's my favourite magazine? That neat Beretta blue metal one which reloads automatically.'

'I'm a man of convictions. Mainly for drink-driving, so far as I remember.'

'My buddies liked America so much – they bought the country.'

'People say, what's the one thing you've got that others haven't which qualifies you to be President? Easy. Dick Cheney.'

'Some people say I only got this job thanks to my dad. That's rubbish. I only got this job thanks to my brother.'

Ways to spot George W. Bush is paranoid

He's the only man in the world with a National Missile Defence duvet.

Secret service men frisk Laura at bedtime. 'Nothing personal honey.'

When the priest told Bush, 'Jesus loves you' – he was held for questioning to find out how he knew.

Bush insists on surveillance photography whenever the Chinese takeaway lad delivers a meal.

On a British visit, Bush sent back his toad-in-the-hole – ''cos there's some goddam sausages hidin' in there ...'

Bush smashed his shaving mirror when 'it kept looking at me in a really creepy way.'

Bush won't take a dump without flushing all the relevant papers down the pan afterwards.

Bush used a speak-your-weight machine then had the FBI arrest it for knowing too much.

Even his gun is bullet proof.

He thinks everyone on the planet is out to get him. To be fair that's not paranoia, that's probably just good judgement.

George W. Bush personal bumper stickers

If you can read this sticker, it's more than I can

My other missile's a nuke

A fool and his money – are now President

Honk if you want to put Cheney back in hospital

Conserve water – use gasoline

If at first you don't succeed – call Jeb

If the earth core's a rockin' – it's a treaty I'm blockin'

Shit happens – ask Al Gore

KIY – Presidents Supporting Dyslexics

Earth first – then we fuck up the universe

Ways to spot Dubya's a corporate puppet

He's wooden, wears a fixed grin and used to spend a lot of time out of his box.

He never starts a speech about the environment until the cheque's cleared.

The White House website now accepts Star Spangled Banner ads.

Thanks to corporate campaign funding, the Bill of Rights has been paid in full.

He's just renamed the Empire 'Swoosh' Building.

The CEO of ExxonMobil has the spare set of keys to the White House.

It's now an official requirement for all Americans to salute the logo.

Bush now regularly opens speeches with the words, 'Congratulations, you may already have won a prize.'

He's now advertising Missile Defence, 'As seen in the new Lara Croft movie.'

He's dumped 'God Bless America' in favour of 'And now a word from our sponsors.'

Reasons Dubya wants a Son of Star Wars missile shield.

In space, no-one can hear you scream. 'Take that Commie motherfuckers!'

He's getting bored with that USA-China virtual war CD-rom Rumsfeld gave him.

'This world ain't big enough for *two* Rogue States…'

Only with a defence shield will Americans be able to sleep peacefully in their reinforced undergound bunkers.

It will get Dubya one up on Clinton. 'He was never able to stop an explosion once he'd entered boost phase.'

He insists spin-off merchandise sales alone will help stimulate the economy.

No-one's had the heart to tell him *Men In Black*
isn't a documentary.

Dubya has always wanted one of those really cool
passes that says 'Access All Areas – Of the Planet.'

(sing) 'War. Huh. Good God y'all. What is it good
for? Absolutely everyone involved with the Bush
administration ... '

'Them foreign folk's real scary, now pass me my
banjo Laura!'

Dubya's favourite Bible passages

Let he who is without sin – sign the next death warrant.

The beautiful passage where Jesus disappears into the awesome unspoilt wilderness – and spends the next 40 days digging it up for oil.

The bit where God rested on the second, third, fourth, fifth, sixth and seventh days.

Jesus turns the water into wine – then foolishly agrees to drive everyone back to his place.

Noah builds the ark, looks at George W. Bush and says, 'Understand global warming now you stupid w****r?'

The famous passage where Jesus arrives with five loaves and two fishes. The Republicans demand a recount and eventually everyone ends up getting stuffed.

Jesus says, 'Take up thy bed and walk – and if I catch you in here again, Mr Clinton, you'll be sorry.'

God commands Adam and Eve to eat from the trees in the Garden. Adam says, 'What trees? All I can see is a drive-in burger bar.'

Jesus enters the temple, sees the moneylenders – then winks and asks them for a massive campaign donation.

The seventh day. God rested, looked at the Earth he had created and said, 'All it needs now is a system of space-based weapons of mass destruction.'

George W. Bush is so insensitive...

He thinks the Kyoto Accord is a new Honda hatchback.

He was asked to sign a death warrant and said, 'Would you like a photo with that?'

He agreed to host the next carbon emissions summit – at Buck's Texan Drive-in Barbecue and Grill.

He prefers dolphin unfriendly tuna.

He attended an electrocution and exclaimed, 'That reminds me, I must get some jump leads for the limo...'

When an inner city council asked what they could build to benefit the kids – Bush suggested a drive-by shooting range.

71

He saw *Armageddon* and really hated that bit at the end where they save the planet.

He went to a 'Save The Whale' rally and took his barbecue tongs – just in case.

When Cheney came out of hospital his first words were 'Thank God you're back Dick – the press have been trying to stitch me up.'

He sent Al Gore a Christmas gift – it was a Chadvent calendar.

Highlights of when Dubya met the Japanese Prime Minister

Relief all round when PM Junichiro Koizumi didn't insist on an anti-vomit defence shield.

Koizumi gave Dubya a Bonsai tree. Bush says, 'Not bad buddy. But back in Texas we've got Bonsai trees a thousand times bigger than this.'

Everyone laughed at the funny pronunciations – then stopped when the Japanese guy started talking.

Dubya realised Koizumi hadn't seen *Pearl Harbour* and said, 'In that case I won't spoil the movie by telling you the ending.'

The chef asked George W. Bush how he liked his sushi – 'Burned to a crisp my friend.'

Dubya was asked what he thought of the pickled cabbage – 'She's my daughter and I'm standing by her.'

The press asked for a translator – they couldn't understand a word Dubya was saying.

Shock when Koizumi called Bush an underhand tosser – relief when they realised he meant Dubya's baseball pitching technique.

Bush proposed a toast to his favourite people, 'the Japanesians.'

Dubya radiates warmth – Koizumi says last time the Americans dropped in on the Japanese unannounced, that's not all they radiated.

Things you'll NEVER hear George W. Bush say

'Checkmate.'

'No grits for me, I'll have the roquette salad.'

'Does anyone mind if I switch *COPS* off – I want to play my new Shostakovich CD.'

'You know, I find too many deer heads detract from the interior decor.'

'Nope, no more for me – I'm driving.'

'Frankly I thought Graceland was a tad tacky.'

'No way are we keeping firearms in this

household.'
'Laura honey – did you mail that donation to Greenpeace?'

'Excuse me – I'm looking for the Philosophy section.'

'Jeb – I want you to keep counting till you get it right.'

Dubya's favourite ways to celebrate Thanksgiving

He takes a good long look at the big old bird with the turkey neck and says, 'I love you mom!'

He gets brother Jeb to come round and organise charades – just like he did in the Florida elections.

The whole family play musical chairs – since dad threw up on the Japanese Prime Minister, no-one likes to sit next to him at dinner.

Barbara asks Dubya to say Grace – 'Because it's one of the few words he can pronounce properly.'

Barbara bakes a pie – George W. says could she make it a bit taller.

The twins organise party games like 'Pass the Parcel' and 'Pin the Tail on the Dad'.

They play Scrabble – Dubya's great at games where you have to jumble up all your letters.

Dubya sits down with the vegetables saying, 'Dad, Donny, Henry, Dick. You guys ran the country before – now do it again for me!'

He produces a crate of Bourbon, two crates of Tequila and three barrels of beer saying, 'Jenna, that's the last time I tidy up your room.'

Dubya enjoys the simple pleasures. Running around the lawn, fetching a stick – and peeing up against the cherry tree.

Reasons George W. Bush loves family values

Because family comes first. And even if family comes second – brother Jeb can always organise a recount.

Family is the foundation of the nation and children are the proof – in Jenna's case 40 per cent proof.

George W. Bush believes the nuclear family is much better than the traditional weapons-based family.

As we say in Texas, 'There's nothing like being with family and loved ones.' In some cases they're the same people.

Family is the well-spring of love and harmony – as Dubya was saying only last week at the Biochemical Weapons briefing meeting.

Dubya says parents can give children something
no-one else can provide – in his case a job for life.

Because when things get tough you can always
count on your brother.

There's nothing like the heartwarming patter of tiny
feet – as they run screaming to avoid the latest
anti-ballistic missile test blast.

Marriage is the foundation stone – of the
multi-billion pound wedding industry.

Living in a nuclear family means one day Dubya
may even stop pronouncing it nuke-u-lar!'

Ways to tell George W. Bush is dyslexic

He thinks being President is as easy as
a...c...b.

He only plays Scrabble with blank discs.

He asked Mike Tyson for a 'flu jab.

He thinks the thesaurus is a character from
Jurassic Park 3.

He tried to hire Secret Service bodyguards from
C&A.

He went to a fish restaurant and ordered
Salman Rushdie.

His favourite film is *The Best Little Warehouse In Texas*.

He went to a toga party dressed as a goat.

He got a ticket for trying to park in an erogenous zone.

He went into his local Gap and tried to nuke the chinos.

Ways to tell George W. Bush is out of his depth

He still has to read the manual before going to work.

He thinks Ja Ja Binks is the capital of Algeria.

He met with the World Bank and asked to borrow some cash for a patio extension.

At State Functions he stares at his private bodyguards and tries to make them giggle.

Only meets with Donald Rumsfeld to talk about 'Son of Star Wars' if he can take his action figures.

He heard that the Senate had agreed a foreign aid package and offered to ask Laura to wrap it.

He cries and sucks his thumb whenever Cheney's
rushed into hospital.

He was the first ever President to moon out of the
window of Air Force One.

He went to the UN and asked for Shania Twain on
his translation headphones.

When asked, 'What are America's geopolitical and
economic stratagems for the next decade?'
he replied, 'Can I phone a friend?'

Bush Administration souvenir gifts

The George W. Bush watch.
It's got two faces but still can't tell the time.

The Dick Cheney watch.
Dodgy ticker and battery powered.

The George W. Bush jacket.
It's a bomber with deep pockets.

The George W. Bush bookmark.
(guaranteed unused).

250 million mugs.
Commemorates the American electorate.

George W. Bush celebration beer.
Alcoholic with a big head.

The Dick Cheney tray.
(carries one big mug).

George W. Bush pen.
Guaranteed exact replica of the one he *doesn't* use
to sign world treaties.

★

George W. Bush lighter.
Runs on oil, fits easily into any businessman's
pocket.

★

Please note – the Donald Rumsfeld plates were
cancelled due to a misunderstanding. He said
'Bone China,' they said, 'Screw America.'

George W. Bush perfect party tips

Dubya insists on good loud music – back in Texas
they call him Frat Boy Grim.

Make sure you've got music to keep old and young
happy. Dubya loves that Eminem track – 'The Real
Slim Cheney'.

Killer cocktails. Dubya doesn't drink, but he likes
his guests to have fun. Try 'Fizzy Math',
'Jenna and Tonic' or 'Rumsfeld Punch'.

People say Dubya's not environmentally conscious.
Rubbish – he often shares a jacuzzi with close
friends.

Have good fresh food. Dubya likes stuff he can
easily get his mouth round – so basically that's
anything with one syllable.

Dubya relaxes guests with affectionate nicknames.
For example, the Pope is 'Mr Dribble My Name'
while Tony Blair is 'You Limey Kiss-Ass'.

Leave politics at the front door. Especially
controversial matters like execution. As Dubya
says, 'It's hardly a matter of life and death.'

When things get boring, Dubya produces Tia
Maria. She's a Mexican maid but also plays guitar.

Dubya won't order pizza. His most recent deep-pan
experience was watching Jenna throw up in the
bathroom.

For God's sake don't ask Rumsfeld to blow up the
balloons (last time someone said that he launched
fifteen intercontinental ballistic missiles).

George W. Bush epitaphs

What now Dick?

Dancing permitted after 6.00p.m.

Here lies George W. Bush...again.

This way up.

First Phase – National Compost Defence Shield.

Here I lie two feet under,
What d'you know?
Another blunder.

At last he's recycling.

Under this sod – another one.

Keep digging – you could strike oil.

Here's mud in your eye Dubya!

6

DUBYA DUBYA DUBYA

The best of the net

'Will the highways on the internet become more few?' **GWB**

'Ma,' said George W. Bush on the phone, 'I beat Al Gore, I'm President!'

'Honestly?' asked Barbara Bush.

'Ma! Why bring that up at a time like this?'

Ralph Nader, Albert Gore and George W. Bush went to a fitness spa for some fun and relaxation. After a stimulating healthy lunch, all three decided to visit the men's room and found a strange looking gent sitting at the entrance who said, 'Welcome. Be sure to check out our newest feature – a mirror which, if you look into it and say something truthful, your greatest wish will come true. However, if you say something false, you will be sucked into the mirror to live in a void of nothingness for all eternity!'

All three men quickly entered and went straight up to the mirror.

Ralph Nader said, 'I think I'm the most truthful of us three.' In an instant the oil industry issued a press release to say it was changing to Wind Power.

Albert Gore stepped up to the mirror and said, 'I think I'm the most ambitious of us three.' Suddenly he found the keys to the White House in his hands.

George W. Bush looked into the mirror and said, 'I think...' and was promptly propelled into eternity...

Bill Clinton, Al Gore and George W. Bush died and found themselves standing on the other side of the Jordan River, looking across at the promised land. The Archangel Michael was standing on the other side and shouted over to them, 'Contrary to what you have been taught, each of you will have to wade across the Jordan River.' As Michael saw their perplexed looks, he reassured them by saying, 'Don't worry. You will sink only proportionally according to the damage you have done on earth. The more the damage, the further you will sink into the water.'

The three American political figures looked at one another, trying to determine who should be the first brave soul to cross the Jordan River. Finally Al Gore volunteered to go first. Slowly he began to wade out into the river, and slowly the water began to get higher and higher, reaching to his waist. Al began to sweat, thinking that all of his sins were coming back to haunt him. He was beginning to wonder if he would ever see the other side. Finally, after what seemed liked an eternity, he began to emerge on the river's bank.

As he made the other side, he looked behind him to see which one of the other brave souls was going next. A shock of surprise registered on his face, as he saw George W. Bush almost in the middle of the river and only his ankles barely touching the water. He turned to Michael and exclaimed, 'I know George W. Bush. Dubya is an old colleague of mine, and he has sinned much, much more than that!'

Before the Archangel Michael could reply, Bush shouted back, 'It's OK Al – I'm standing on Clinton's shoulders!'

Dick Cheney was feeling heart pangs while out walking in Washington with George W. Bush. Dubya calls 911 on his mobile. The 911 operator tells Dubya she will send someone out right away adding, 'Where is your exact location?'

Dubya – who doesn't spend much time in Washington – looks at Cheney and says, 'Where are we Dick?' By now, poor Cheney is lying gasping on the floor, hardly moving.

Cheney groans, 'Massachusetts Avenue.' Dubya tells the operator who says, 'Can you spell that for me?'

There's a very long pause. Dubya replies, 'Look, how 'bout if I drag him back to the White House and you pick him up from there?'

George W. Bush was in court charged with parking his car in a restricted area. The judge asked him if he had anything to say in his defence. 'They should not put up such misleading notices,' said Dubya. 'It said, FINE FOR PARKING HERE.'

Q: Why doesn't George W. Bush get haemorrhoids?
A: Because he's a perfect asshole.

Q: What do you call Bush voters who aren't millionaires?
A: Suckers.

Q: How do you tell the Bush/Quayle administration from the Bush/Cheney administration?
A: This time the stupid one's in charge.

★

This old guy says, 'You know, this Bush? What he is, is a post-turtle.'

His friend says, 'What the hell is a post-turtle?'

'Well, let's say you're driving down a country road and you see a turtle balanced on a fence post. That's a post-turtle. You know he didn't get there by himself, he doesn't belong there, he can't get anything done while he's up there, and you just want to help the poor thing down.'

The friend says, 'Back in Texas, we'd just throw a rock at it.' (Gary Goodrow)

Back when George W. Bush was footloose and fancy free in Texas, a state trooper pulled him over when he was out driving. He looks at Dubya and says, 'Got any ID?'

Dubya grins and says, ''bout what?'

A reporter cornered George W. Bush at a press conference. 'Many say the only reason you were elected for President is due to the enormous power and influence of your father.'
'That notion is ridiculous!' said George W. 'He only had one vote didn't he?'

Q: What do George W. and Laura Bush have in common?
A: They're both rumoured to have blown a little dope.

A conservative is a guy who kicks a bum in the gutter shouting, 'Get a job!' A compassionate conservative is a guy who kicks a bum in the gutter shouting, 'Get a job – here's the small ads.'

While visiting England, George W. Bush is invited for tea with the Queen. Bush asks what her philosophy is. The Queen replies that it's to surround herself with intelligent advisers. George W. asks how she knows if they are truly intelligent. 'By asking them the right questions,' says the Queen. 'Allow me to demonstrate.' She phones Tony Blair and says, 'Mr Prime Minister, please answer this question. Your mother has a child, and your father has a child, and this child is not your brother or sister. Who is it?'

Tony Blair immediately responds, 'Certainly, the child would be me, ma'am.'

'Correct. Thank you and good-bye, Mr Prime Minister,' says the Queen. She hangs up and says, 'Did you get that, George?'

'Yes, Your Majesty. Thanks a lot. I'll definitely be using that one!'

Bush returns to Washington and decides he better put the Chairman of the Senate Foreign Relations Committee to the test. He summons Jesse Helms to the White House and says, 'Senator Helms, answer a question for me. Uhh, your mother has a child, and your father has a child, and this child is not your brother or your sister. Who is it?'

Helms looks really stumped and says, 'Can I think about it and get back to you?' Bush agrees, and Helms leaves.

Helms calls a meeting of Republican senators, and they puzzle over the question for several hours, but

nobody can come up with an answer. Finally, in desperation, Helms calls Colin Powell and explains his problem. Senator Helms says, 'Now lookee here, son, your mother has a child, and your father has a child, and this child is not your brother or your sister. Who is it?'

Powell answers immediately, 'It's me, of course, you dumb cracker.' Much relieved, Senator Helms rushes back to the White House and exclaims, 'George, I know the answer! I know who it is! It's Colin Powell!'

Mr. Bush replies in total disgust, 'Wrong, you dumb shit, it's Tony Blair!'

George Bush and Cheney are having lunch at a diner near the White House. Cheney orders the 'Heart Healthy' salad. Bush leans over to the waitress and says, 'Honey, could I have a quickie?'

Horrified she says, 'Mr President, I thought your administration would bring a new era of moral rectitude to the White House. Now I see I was wrong,' and marches off.

Cheney leans over and says, 'George, I think it's pronounced "QUICHE".'

George W. Bush is truly ignorant of the affairs of state. He thinks Roe v. Wade are options for crossing the Mississippi river.

George W. Bush said he is going to run his own campaign and be his own man. What's really amazing is he said this while Cheney was drinking a glass of water.

One day Dubya decides he wants to learn to sky dive so he talks to Cheney who has done it before. Cheney agrees to teach him how so they go up in Air Force One somewhere over Texas and Cheney says to Dubya, 'Jump out and pull your rip cord. I'll be right behind you and we'll go down together. OK?'

Bush jumps out and pulls his ripcord and starts floating down. Cheney jumps out, immediately has a heart attack and flies past Dubya.

Bush sees Cheney dropping like a stone and, undoing his parachute, screams, 'So ya wanna race, do ya?' (www.allhatnocattle.net)

Bill Clinton, Al Gore and George W. Bush are sent to face a firing squad in a small South American country. Clinton is forced up against the wall (not for the first time). Just as the squad begins to take aim, Clinton shouts at the top of his voice, 'Hurricane!'

To his immense relief the firing squad panics and run off in all directions, allowing him to scale the wall and make his escape.

Eventually order is restored, and next up is Gore. Once again, just as the guns are pointing at his head, Gore yells for all he is worth, 'Tornado!'

The squad dash for cover and Gore follows in the footsteps of Clinton as fast as his legs can carry him.

Things once again calm down and the squad return, untie Dubya and place him up against the wall. Dubya knows he's only got one chance to save his skin. As the guns are loaded and pointed, Bush smiles to himself then screams at the top of his voice, 'Fire!'

Einstein dies and goes to heaven. Saint Peter tells him, 'You look like Einstein, but you've NO idea the lengths some people will go to to sneak in here. Can you prove who you really are?'

Einstein ponders for a few seconds and asks, 'Could I have a blackboard and some chalk?' Saint Peter snaps his fingers and a blackboard and chalk instantly appear. Einstein then describes with arcane mathematics and symbols his theory of relativity. Saint Peter is impressed. 'Welcome to heaven, Einstein!' he says.

Next to arrive is Picasso. Once again, Saint Peter asks for credentials. Picasso replies, 'Mind if I use that blackboard and chalk?' Saint Peter says, 'Go ahead.'

Picasso erases Einstein's equations and sketches a truly stunning mural with just a few strokes of chalk.

Saint Peter claps. 'Surely you are the great artist you claim to be. Come on in!'

Then George W. Bush arrives. Saint Peter says 'Einstein and Picasso both managed to prove their identity. How can you prove yours?'

George W. looks bewildered and says, 'Who are Einstein and Picasso?' Saint Peter sighs and says, 'OK George, come in.'

At least George W. Bush is faithful to his wife. In fact the only other people he's been in bed with are the gun lobby, the oil business and the tobacco industry.

During the election campaign Bush was caught on stage muttering to Dick Cheney about a journalist. 'That's Adam Clymer – major league asshole.' It's Dubya's finest ever achievement – producing a story with the words Bush, Dick and asshole in the same sentence.

Dick Cheney gets a call from his 'boss' Dubya. 'I've got a problem,' says George.

'What's the matter?' asks Cheney.

'Well, you told me to keep busy in the Oval Office, so, I've bought this jigsaw puzle, but it's too hard. None of the pieces fit together and I can't find any edges.'

'What's the picture of?' asks Cheney.

'It's a big rooster,' says Dubya.

'All right,' sighs Cheney, 'I'll come over and have a look.'

So he leaves his desk and heads over to the Oval Office. The secretary lets Cheney into the Office and Dubya calls him over to the coffee table. He points and shows him the unfinished jigsaw.

Cheney looks at the jigsaw, turns to Dubya and says, 'For Christ's sake, George – put the corn flakes back in the box.'

7

FRIEND OR FOE?
Who says what about Dubya

'When I'm talking about myself, and when he's talking about myself, all of us are talking about me.' GWB

'President Bush took a trip to England. In preparation for the visit he spent hours trying to learn a few words of the language.' *Jay Leno*

'President George W. Bush addressed a conference of NATO officials on the validity of his proposed missile shield. The pitch was met with serious scepticism.

Well, let's face it, Bush can't even prevent his own daughters from getting bombed.' *Craig Kilborn*

'George W. Bush – the only man on the planet who thinks the Taliban is a rock group.' *Paul Begala*

'I like to think of him as Drinky McDumbass.' *Bill Maher*

'I'm not making this up, but in Florida, when they counted the ballots, they held each one up to see if any light went through it . . . just like with Bush's head!' *Jay Leno*

'The good news is the White House is now giving George W. Bush intelligence briefings...some of these jokes actually write themselves.' *David Letterman*

'Bush has a new slogan. It's "Reformer with Results" which I think is a big improvement on the old one – "Dumb Guy with Connections".' *David Letterman*

'George W. Bush invokes a lot of Bible imagery. He says Jesus also had twenty missing years and never held a job he couldn't get through his dad.' *Jay Leno*

'Bush could have the first Presidential Library where it's all books on tape.' *Jay Leno*

'Republicans called the Bush-Cheney ticket the "Wizard of Oz" ticket. One needs a heart and the other needs a brain.' *Jay Leno*

'He is the President, although old habits die hard. It's funny with Bush. Now whenever the Secret Service knocks on the door, he keeps flushing stuff down the toilet.' *Jay Leno*

'Dubya's appointed Senator John Ashcroft as Attorney General. No one expects Ashcroft to have any indiscretions. He's a fundamentalist, doesn't believe in drinking, doesn't believe in smoking, doesn't believe in partying. The question is – how the hell did he meet George W. Bush?' *Jay Leno*

'Hillary Clinton met with incoming First Lady Laura Bush. Actually, Laura Bush does have something in common with Hillary Clinton. She also has no idea what her husband is doing in the Oval Office.' *Jay Leno*

'I have something else to ask you, to ask every American. I ask you to pray for this great nation.' *George W. Bush*

'We're way ahead of you, George.' *Jon Stewart*

'On Saturday, amidst pomp and extenuating circumstance, Bush was sworn in as leader of the free world. The only non-traditional element in this inauguration is the winner was watching it from Tennessee.' *Jon Stewart*

'I could never be the President. Think about it. I've abused cocaine, I've been arrested, I'm not a very smart guy. It's a big joke to think people would want someone like me just because his dad was President.' *Charlie Sheen, asked on* Saturday Night Live *if he'd like to take over dad Martin's job in TV show* The West Wing

'The water has really cleared up here in New York City. You know the East River, it used to have a head on it. We have George W. Bush to thank for this new clean water. Yeah, it's coming down from the melted ice caps.' *David Letterman*

'President Bush admitted today that he is a friend of the electrical industry.

He said, "I owe them a lot – in fact if it wasn't for the electrical college, I wouldn't be President".' *Jay Leno*

'As I like to say, the man is not bilingual. He is bi-ignorant.' *Molly Ivins*

'Overall Bush's European trip was an overwhelming success. Not once did he get separated from his group.' *David Letterman*

'Karl Rove is in hot water over a meeting he had with Intel executives, a company he owns $100,000 worth of stock in. Democrats say he could face ethics charges, but Rove says the meeting was good for America. Apparently, Intel is working on a new chip that would allow President Bush to process information faster.' *Jay Jaroch*

'Former President George Bush has invited former Russian President Boris Yeltsin to visit him in the United States. This is a new strategy for the Bush family – to hang out with people who drink more than they do.' *Jay Leno*

'Bush says going to Europe isn't much of an adjustment for him. In a lot of these countries they drink a lot and drive on the other side of the road, just like he used to do.' *Jay Leno*

'Even Dubya's loyal defenders say he's a few beans short of a full burrito.' *Paul Begala*

'Governor Jeb Bush of Florida announced he was running for re-election. Not only did he announce he was running for re-election, he also announced what his final vote count would be.' *Jay Leno*

'George W. Bush is a man who does not know how much he does not know, and seems in no rush to find out.' *Frank Rich*

'Some good news on the Bush girls. It seems that Jenna Bush is taking up a new musical instrument. She's learning how to play the Breathalyzer.' *Jay Leno*

'I think Bush is basically a good man. He doesn't know the meaning of the word intolerance – then again he doesn't know what continent Mexico is on or where he was for a year in the National Guard.' *Paul Begala*

'Jenna Bush was caught trying to buy a drink in Austin with a fake ID. It was her second alcohol incident in a month. She must be extra careful from now on. Under federal law, it's "Three Strikes and You're President".' *Argus Hamilton*

'Yesterday up in New Haven President Bush gave the Commencement address and they gave him an honorary law degree. So that means now he's an honorary lawyer, just like he's an honorary President.' *David Letterman*

'President Bush has appointed a new drug policy director, a gentleman by the name of John Walters who is known for his tough approach to fighting drugs. Walters will be President Bush's first drug adviser since, well, since Captain Acid two doors down at College.' *Jay Leno*

'The White House announced that President Bush recently submitted to a urine test. Not surprisingly, before taking the test, the President wrote the correct answers on his hand.' *Conan O'Brien*

'This weekend George W. Bush will become the first President in United States history to deliver his weekly radio address from the Oval Office entirely in Spanish. I guess he realized, "Look, this English thing isn't working out for me".' *Jay Leno*

'In the Clinton administration we worried the President would open his zipper, and in the Bush administration, they worry the President will open his mouth.' *Former Clinton adviser James Carville*

'George W. Bush has named his old college fraternity brother as an ambassador to China. Apparently he's fluent in Mandarin Chinese. In fact, he gave Bush a Chinese nickname – Dim Son.' *Jay Leno*

'George W. Bush didn't mind the fact that he arrived in New York in sweltering heat – things cooled down nicely when he got his usual frosty reception.' *David Letterman*

'*The Weakest Link* is a fascinating program. They ask a bunch of people questions and they keep getting rid of the dumbest person, so just the smartest person is left. It is kind of the opposite way we elect a President.' *Jay Leno*

'George W. Bush is more stupid than Ronald Reagan put together.' *Adapted from a line by Matt Groening*